THE DREAM OF GERONTIUS

John Henry Newman

ST PAULS

cover illustration:
Portrait of John Henry Newman
by A R Venables, 1868
by courtesy of the Oxford Oratory

original edition published by
FAMILY PUBLICATIONS
77 Banbury Road, Oxford, England
(ISBN 1-871217-32-6)

US edition published by
ST PAULS / Alba House
2187 Victory Boulevard
Staten Island, NY 10314-6603

ISBN 0-8189-0907-2

This edition is for sale in USA, Canada and US territories only

printed in England by
The Cromwell Press, Trowbridge

CONTENTS

Illustrations

John Henry Newman,
the Richmond Portrait (1845)

PREFACE

This splendid edition of *The Dream of Gerontius* makes available to contemporary readers a gem of Catholic literature that was lost in the shuffle after Vatican II. The perennial significance of *The Dream* is attested to by the fact that several of the world's greatest symphony orchestras have recently celebrated the centenary of the first performance of Elgar's incredible musical interpretation of this epic poem written by the venerable Cardinal John Henry Newman. I had already arranged with Alba House for a new edition when I discovered this English publication. Alba House, which has brought out so many helpful spiritual books, agreed to work along with Family Publications of Oxford who had recently put out this English edition. Bravo!

You may be surprised that so many readers are now suddenly interested in the Catholic doctrine on purgatory, which is the theme of the poem. This very sensible and consoling teaching on the experience of the soul after death, preparing it to receive the fullness of salvation merited by Christ alone, has been all but forgotten. Sadly, one can attend funerals that are ersatz canonizations of some poor souls who could obviously use a prayer. Contemporary Christians have forgotten or never known that the Fathers of the Church as early as the third century, and early ecclesiastical writers as well, have been urging Christians to prayerfully help their beloved dead on the journey to the Beatific Vision. The rejection of prayers for the dead and of the notion of purification after death were totally novel ideas of the Protestant Reformers. They arrived at their conclusion as a result of their belief in double predestination, that odd thought that salvation does not require any cooperation of the individual. In East and West, Christians have prayed for the dead, thus accepting the idea of purgatory, since earliest Christian times. In *The Dream*, Cardinal Newman brings together scripture, theology, tradition, the revelations of the mystics (especially St Catherine of Genoa) and his own incomparable intellect to provide a beautiful but awesome glance at the first moments after death. *The Dream* is an adventure in faith. Study it and life will make a lot more sense to you, and so will death. Make the effort to deal with its slightly archaic speech and the old ideas about the Last Judgment and you will surely be a deeper and better Christian when you get finished. Like any great classic *The Dream* will remain with you for good and you will see life and death in a different perspective.

Fr Benedict J Groeschel, CFR
Author of *The Journey Toward God*

FOREWORD

Since my recent appointment as Archbishop of Birmingham, I have already come to realise the great historical riches which are to be found within the Archdiocese.

On visiting St George's Parish, Worcester, I was interested to learn that the young Edward Elgar had been organist there, as had his father before him. I was aware too of the close association of Cardinal Newman with so many aspects of Birmingham life, particularly the Maryvale Institute and Oscott College, and of course the Oratory which he established in 1848, and where he lived, worked and prayed for over forty years.

The natural talent and religious sentiment of these two great men came together in the creation of Elgar's masterpiece, *The Dream of Gerontius*. It had its first performance at the Town Hall in Birmingham, on 3 October 1900; thus, as we enter into the celebration of the bicentenary of Newman's birth, there have already been performances to commemorate the centenary of Elgar's work in Birmingham and elsewhere.

I am very grateful to all who have co-operated in the production of this new edition of Newman's poem. The introductions that the book contains, to Cardinal Newman and to Sir Edward Elgar, are both informative and attractive. I hope that this new edition will widen the appreciation of the religious genius of the poem, and serve to enhance recognition of the contribution that Cardinal Newman has made to Catholic life in this country.

✠*Vincent Nichols*
Archbishop of Birmingham

1

The waves of death rose about me;
the torrents of destruction assailed me;
the snares of the grave entangled me;
the traps of death confronted me.

In my anguish I cried to the Lord;
I cried to my God for help.
From his temple he heard my voice;
my cry came to his ears . . .

From on high he reached down and seized me;
He drew me forth from the mighty waters.
He snatched me from my powerful foe,
from my enemies whose strength I could not match.

They assailed me in the day of my misfortune,
but the Lord was my support,
He brought me forth into freedom,
he saved me because he loved me.

Psalm 17

INTRODUCTION

The Dream of Gerontius is a dramatic poem which portrays the death of an old man and what happens to his soul as he enters into eternity. It is therefore a poem that is coloured by the beliefs of the author.

John Henry Newman was born on 21 February 1801 and died on 11 August 1890. He was baptized soon after his birth, according to the rites of the Church of England, but was to die many years later as a Cardinal of the Catholic Church. After a boyhood conversion at the age of fifteen, Newman went to Oxford, where he later became a Fellow of Oriel College, Vicar of the University Church and one of the leaders of the Oxford Movement, the aim of which was to renew the spirit of the Church of England along apostolic and Catholic lines. He was received into the Catholic Church in 1845, and settled in Birmingham. After ordination as a Catholic priest he founded the first English Congregation of the Oratory in Birmingham, and set up the Catholic University of Ireland in Dublin and the Oratory public school in Birmingham.

He was created Cardinal by Pope Leo XIII in 1879 'for his services ... and for long years rendered to religion'. He wrote extensively, both as an Anglican and as a Catholic – theological, philosophical, historical, controversial and literary works, in defence of Christianity and Revealed Religion; his *Parochial and Plain Sermons* were especially influential. He was therefore a Christian all his life, even though his spiritual pilgrimage led him to leave the church of his boyhood and become a Roman Catholic.

Newman's Christianity influenced not only his writing of the *Dream,* but also the way it was received by the public. Since Newman's time there have been many changes in English society, and most of all in the beliefs of the citizens of this realm; but, in the nineteenth century, England could still call itself a Christian land. Throughout the century churches continued to be built and enlarged all over the country by Anglicans, Free Churchmen, and Roman Catholics alike. Along with this outward manifestation of church life, there went a number of Christian beliefs which were held by the commonality of men. Probably the strongest among these were: the existence of God, the fact of an afterlife, God's providential care of each one of us, and trust in the atoning death of Our Lord Jesus Christ.

It was this common core of belief which helped to give *The Dream of Gerontius* such universal appeal when it was first published, and which gained for the author an equally general approbation, forgetful of the denominational rivalries of the period. However, when looked at closely, the whole poem is about the death of an old, practising Catholic, surrounded at his deathbed by Catholic friends: they utter Catholic prayers culled from the prayers for the dying in the Roman ritual, they have called in the priest to administer the Last Sacraments, and they believe confidently in the intercession of Our Lady and all the angels and Saints. The power of the poem, with its dramatic depiction of the passage of the soul from this life to eternity, is such that Christians of all persuasions felt and still feel at home with it.

The Christians of the Victorian period likewise felt a similar sympathy with the author of the poem himself, because they knew him as a man who was prepared to follow the truth wherever it led him, regardless of the consequences and its effect upon his own personal prospects. He was a man whose greatness and his loyalty to Christ were such that he commanded the love and respect of men from all walks of life, all kinds of churchmanship, and all persuasions of religious belief, because of his undoubted integrity. The general public was particularly aware of this in 1865, when *The Dream* was written. 1864 had seen the production of Newman's spiritual autobiography, *Apologia pro Vita Sua,* in which his sincerity had stood out so clearly. Furthermore, because the *Apologia* had first appeared in serial form in the press, this had gained for its author a much wider public recognition than might otherwise have been the case. Newman's name was still very much in the public mind when *The Dream* was first published.

In our time *The Dream of Gerontius* has become popular and well-known through being set to music by Sir Edward Elgar; but in Newman's time it was as *religious* poetry that it compelled attention. Newman's own comments in a letter to Lady Chatterton of 18 September 1870[1] are to the point:

> As to my own Gerontius, it was not the versification which sold it, but the subject. It is a RELIGIOUS subject which appeals strongly to the feelings of everyone. I heard of one farmer who was a most unlikely man to care about poetry, who took to it when he was ill – it was to him a prayer or meditation. It directed his thoughts to the next world, from no merits of its own, but from its subject . . .

One famous person who used it in this way was the Free Churchman General Gordon, who died in 1884 at the taking

---

1 *Letters and Diaries of John Henry Newman*, OUP (31 vols); XXV, p 209.

of Khartoum. He used the poem in his very last moments, marking with a pencil all the passages which struck him as bearing on death and prayer. For instance, 'Pray for me, O my friends'; 'Tis death, O loving friends, your prayers – 'tis he . . . '; 'Prepare to meet thy God'; 'Use well the interval . . . Now that the hour is come, my fear is fled'. Newman was very touched to know about this incident, because he had himself been thinking about Gordon, and had cut a little map out of *The Times* newspaper and stuck it on his cupboard door to remind him of the campaign (the press-cutting is still there to this day in Newman's room). Gladstone, who was a devout Anglican, wrote to Newman on 1 January 1868:

> I own that it seems to me the most remarkable production in its own very high walk since the unapproachable *Paradiso* of Dante, and his less (but not very much less) wonderful *Purgatorio*.[2]

The Presbyterian divine Dr Alexander Whyte said of it:

> *The Dream of Gerontius* was the true copestone for Newman to cut and lay on the literary and religious work of his whole life . . . there is nothing of its kind outside of the *Purgatorio* and the *Paradiso* at all equal to the *Gerontius* for solemnising, enobling and sanctifying powers. It is a poem that everyone should have by heart who has it before him to die!

But the comment that most enlightens us as to the general popularity of the poem among Christians is that of Newman's

---

2 *Letters and Diaries* XXIV p 7

adversary in the period immediately before the writing of *The Dream,* namely Charles Kingsley. He wrote on 2 May 1868 to Sir William Cope:

> I read *The Dream* with awe and admiration. However utterly I may differ from the *entourage* in which Newman's present creed surrounds the central idea, I must feel that the central idea is as true as it is noble, and it, I suppose, is this: the longing of the soul to behold Deity, converted, by the mere act of sight, into a self-abasement so utter, that the soul is ready, even glad, to be hurled back to any depth, to endure any pain, from the moment it becomes aware of God's actual perfection and its own utter impurity and meanness.[3]

Outline of the plot of *The Dream*

Kingsley was right in seizing on the soul's appearance before his Judge as the climax to which the whole plot of the poem leads. Newman, keeping all the while closely to the practice and teaching of the Church, and to all that Scripture – the Revealed Word of God – and Tradition – its interpreter – say, describes what happens to an ordinary soul dying in a state of grace. True it is 'a dream', but it is a 'dream' based on what almighty God has said, and is therefore describing a *real* not an *imaginary* world 'revealed to the eyes of faith'. True, it is a mystery where we have darkness as well as light, but there is enough

---

3 *Charles Kingsley – His Letters* Vol. II 1877 p 270

light for us to be able to see something, and what we see is certain, no mere guess. The angels are real, the fallen angels are real, and so is the disembodied soul.

Gerontius is dying. He feels that he is going and that he will sink back 'into that utter nothingness, of which I came'. Strengthened by the Sacraments and the prayers of friends, he gathers enough energy to make his profession of faith – the necessary condition of salvation, according to Scripture. He does so in the words of the famous hymn 'Firmly I believe and truly'. Despite the frightening last-minute attacks of the demons, he passes into the next life in a state of grace. The disembodied soul is bewildered in his new environment, and seeks for light from his guardian angel, whom he encounters singing a song that announces that he is saved, though not yet enjoying the Beatific Vision:

> My work is done,
> My work is o'er
> And so I come
> Taking it home.
> For the crown is won.
> Alleluia,
> For evermore.

The Angel tells him that he is being carried into the presence of the Judge. They pass first a howling mob of demons, who are however powerless to hurt them; and then, as they draw closer, choirs of angels are heard around the throne singing: 'Praise to the Holiest in the height ...' Finally, as they get nearer still to the Throne, the prayers of his friends on earth arise before the Throne, and the Angel of the Agony, who strengthened Christ in Gethsemane, prays for him. Suddenly, (as the Guardian Angel says), the soul

> ... flies to the dear feet of Emmanuel;
> But, ere it reach them, the keen sanctity,
> Which with its effluence, like a glory clothes
> And circles round the Crucified, has seized,
> and scorched, and shrivelled it, and now it lies,
> Passive and still before the awful Throne.

The soul is safe, 'consumed, yet quickened, by the glance of God'. And then the soul, aware of its own need for purification and perfect holiness before it can see God face to face, sings the beautiful song that is one of the highlights of the whole poem, asking to be sent to Purgatory ...

> Take me away, and in the lowest deep
>   There let me be,
> And there in hope the lone night watches keep,
>   Told out for me.
> There, motionless and happy in my pain,
>   Lone not forlorn,
> There will I sing my sad perpetual strain,
>   Until the morn.
> There will I sing and soothe my stricken breast,
>   Which ne'er can cease
> To throb, and pine, and languish, till possest
>   Of its Sole Peace.
> There will I sing my absent Lord and Love;
>   Take me away,
> That sooner I may rise and go above,
>   And seek Him in the truth of everlasting day.

The poem ends with the Angel taking the Soul to Purgatory as he had asked.

The ideas or beliefs of *The Dream*

We have already pointed out that many of the key ideas and beliefs that come across in *The Dream* were the common property of Christians of all denominations in the nineteenth century, although of course their expression here bears Newman's own stamp upon them. In his other writings, many of these principal beliefs had been worked out in great detail, especially in the sermons preached in Oxford, and published as *Parochial and Plain Sermons*[4]. Many of them attain succinct and final expression in his *Meditations and Devotions*[5], where they are worked out in relation to his own life and mission.

Beliefs such as that in the immortality and uniqueness of each human soul, in the reality of the life of the world to come, and in the Divinity of Our Lord and Saviour Jesus Christ, who was made man for us, date from his boyhood, especially after the conversion that happened to him in the late autumn of 1816. 'When I was fifteen a great change of thought took place in me. I fell under the influences of a definite creed, and received into my intellect impressions of dogma which, through God's mercy, have never been effaced or obscured.' The *Apologia*, from which this quotation comes, was written in 1864. But in 1887 he was still affirming the same unshakeable belief. Writing to the Reverend George T Edwards, an Anglican clergyman, on 24 February 1887, he says:

---

4 Ignatius Press, 1997
5 See *Prayers, Verses and Devotions,* Ignatius Press 1989

What can I say, but that those great and, burning truths, which I learnt when a boy from evangelical teaching, I have found impressed upon my heart with fresh and ever increasing force by the Holy Roman Church? That Church has added to the simple evangelicalism of my first teachers, but it has obscured, diluted, enfeebled nothing of it . . .

On the other hand, his beliefs about Angels, about the Judgement and about exactly what happens to the soul after death, did develop considerably down the years, and certainly this is so with regard to Purgatory, which he accepted wholeheartedly when he became a Catholic, though he had discovered it in the teaching of the Fathers when writing his *Essay on the Development of Doctrine* and earlier.

So far we have spoken principally about the ideas and beliefs that Newman was trying to convey in *The Dream*. These have to do with the life of the world to come, with that Invisible World of which he had written so vividly in his *Parochial and Plain Sermons*[6] (see especially pp 860–868) and which had always had a fascination for him since his earliest childhood.

A brief word must also be said about the means by which the poet sought to convey his thoughts to his audience; on Newman's own showing the poet must not only have something to say, but must also touch the hearts and affections of men and women in saying it. The words in which the ideas are expressed must match their subject. Some authors, like Dante, in trying

---

6 Ignatius Press, 1997

to convey the life of the world to come, have boldly used the sensuous imagery of this world in order to achieve their object. But Newman lays this aside as unsuitable to his purpose and tries rather to convey to us that the afterlife is one which is super-sensuous, where 'this gaudy world has grown pale before the beauty of God's grace', and is one which is peopled by spirits, angels, souls, the Blessed Virgin and the Supreme Judge himself rather than any material realities. So he uses, instead of sensuous imagery, variations in metre, and the use of liturgical language with the thoughts and feelings that this evokes.

> Go forth upon thy journey, Christian soul!
>   Go, from this world! Go, in the name of God
> The Omnipotent Father who created thee!
>   Go, in the name of Jesus Christ, our Lord,
> Son of the Living God, who bled for thee!

He introduces too what one author has called 'the poetry of dogma':

> O wisest love! that flesh and blood
>   Which did in Adam fail,
> Should strive afresh against the foe,
>   Should strive and should prevail.

He uses also that whole plot of the movement of Gerontius' soul towards his Creator and Judge that we have already described. The resulting poetry, of course, lacks something of the earthly imagery of a Wordsworth or of a Dante, but it has its own power; and even if it is not the greatest of the world's poetic masterpieces, it is certainly Newman's greatest poem and it will not be forgotten even in an age of unbelief.

Circumstances of the publication of *The Dream*

1864 had been a trying year for Newman, for it had seen the controversy with Charles Kingsley that ended in Newman writing his *Apologia pro Vita Sua*. It had also seen the birth and demise of his first attempt to found an Oratory in Oxford[7]. These two affairs had used up most of the time he had spare from his community, parochial and school duties at Edgbaston.

Despite this, Newman still found time to encourage a remarkable woman named Fanny Margaret Taylor (1832-1900) in her literary efforts. The daughter of an Anglican clergyman, she went to the Crimea as one of Florence Nightingale's nurses, and while out there was received into the Catholic Church. On returning to her mother she devoted herself to the poor but kept up her writing and, in 1857, published *Eastern Hospitals and English Nurses*, two volumes, giving an unvarnished account of the disgraceful conditions of the military hospitals. In 1862 she became the proprietor of the popular Catholic weekly *The Lamp* and, in 1864, with the help of some Jesuits and of Newman, she founded and edited for the first year a more intellectual Catholic periodical, *The Month*. This publication was then taken over by the Jesuits.

A year or two later, while continuing to write Catholic novels and other books, she founded an order of nuns for the service of the poor, The Poor Servants of the Mother of God, which grew rapidly. It was to help her find copy for her new magazine that *The Dream of Gerontius* was first published in the May and June numbers of *The Month* in 1865.

There has been much speculation among literary critics as to what motivated Newman to write his longest poem at the

---

7 This was not to be achieved until 1990, a hundred years after Newman's death.

age of nearly 64 – and at a time when he was very busy. But we are best to be content with his own explanation of what happened. In a letter to his friend T W Allies, dated 11 October 1865, he writes:

> I assure you I have nothing more to produce of Gerontius. On the 17th January last it came into my head to write it. I really cannot tell how, and I wrote on till it was finished, on small bits of paper. And I could no more write anything else by willing it, than I could fly. I am greatly honoured by the good Nuns of Notre Dame having got their children to act it.[8]

A fortnight or so later on 29 October 1865 he wrote to Lady Charles Thynne:

> I am as much pleased, and half-surprised that you and others should like the Dream of Gerontius. It was written by accident – and it was published by accident. But now that I am encouraged by friends such as yourself, deliberately to commit myself to it, I dare say I shall print it by itself . . .

In fact Newman lost no time in getting it published, and his dedication of the first edition published independently of *The Month* is dated 2 November 1865 – All Souls Day. The dedication was made to Father John Joseph Gordon, the first priest of the Birmingham Oratory to die – and Newman wrote to his brother Philip of the London Oratory:

---

8 *Letters and Diaries*, Vol. XXII

My dear Father Joseph,

I am glad to have done a thing pleasing to you and to your mother – I was prompted to it by that never sleeping remembrance which I have of your dear brother,

> yours affectionately in Christ
> John H Newman of the Oratory

Conclusion

It is hoped that this new edition of *The Dream* will strengthen the faith of all Christian believers as it did in Newman's day and draw them closer together 'in the truth', and that in an age when all kinds of strange notions about the after-life are circulating in society it may, through its poetry and beauty, help to bring men and women back to Christ their Saviour, the true hero of the poem, and to the truth about the life of the world to come that Jesus Christ revealed and hands down to us through his Church.

> *Reverend Gregory Winterton*
> *The Oratory, Birmingham*
> *6 January 2001*

Edward Elgar in 1900

ELGAR'S DREAM

Edward Elgar was born in 1857 at Broadheath, near Worcester where his father had a music shop and was organist at St George's Catholic Church. The young Elgar was a talented violinist; he also played the cello, double-bass, bassoon and trombone, and succeeded his father as organist at St George's in 1885. He gave a copy of Newman's *Dream of Gerontius* to his future wife in 1887 at the time of her mother's death; when he was married two years later at the newly built Brompton Oratory in London he was himself given a copy of the poem as a wedding present by his parish priest from Worcester.

Nearly ten years later he was invited to compose the main new choral work for the Birmingham Triennial Festival in 1900. The Birmingham Festivals were among the most prestigious in Britain, having premiered several important new works at the Birmingham Town Hall, including Mendelssohn's *Elijah* in 1846. Dvorak had been given a German version of Newman's poem with a view to setting it for the 1888 festival, but submitted his *Requiem* instead.

Elgar was already well established as a composer and had recently enjoyed considerable success with his *Enigma Variations* both in England and Germany. It was agreed that he should use Newman's poem, and with the help of the Fathers of the Birmingham Oratory he selected approximately three hundred out of the nine hundred verses as his text. He began work in January 1900 on what was to become his greatest choral and orchestral work, completing it in June, with the full orchestral score in August. He was well pleased with the result, writing at the top of the score the initials for *Ad Maiorem Dei Gloriam* (To the Greater Glory of God). At the end of the score he quoted from Ruskin's *Sesame and Lilies:*

> This is the best of me; for the rest, I ate, and drank, and slept, loved and hated, like another: my life was as the vapour, and is not; but *this* I saw and knew; this, if anything of mine, is worth your memory.

Clearly, greatly moved by the work, he confided in a letter to a friend:

> I think you will find Gerontius far beyond anything I have yet written — I like it ... and have written my own heart's blood into the score.

Preparations for the first performance were beset with problems. In June the Birmingham chorus master was taken ill with pneumonia and died within a few days. Instead of seeking a suitable successor, the former chorus master was brought out of retirement and rehearsals began in August. Scored for three soloists, double chorus and large orchestra, the work was much more complex than the chorus was accustomed to; there were insufficient and inadequate rehearsals and the first performance on 3rd October 1900 was a disaster. Even the distinguished German conductor Hans Richter had underestimated the magnitude of the work and was unable to save the day. He set a slow tempo, but the chorus lost pitch during the *Kyrie* and never fully regained it, and the soloists were not much better.

Elgar was distraught; however, most of the musical commentators present recognised the greatness of the music. The critic in the London *Observer* commented:

> Dr Richter is an orchestral conductor *par excellence*, but his ability to direct performances of English oratorio is open to question ... The shortcomings of the choir were specially to be regretted, because Mr Edward Elgar's sacred cantata *The Dream of Gerontius*, the outcome of eight years' thought, and a choral masterpiece, was presented in so faulty and pointless a manner as to seriously jeopardise its success.

Further performances followed throughout Britain and in Germany and the USA. It was particularly well received in Düsseldorf in 1902, where the composer Richard Strauss proposed a toast to 'the welfare and success of the first English progressivist, Meister Edward Elgar'. Elgar himself conducted the performance at the Three Choirs Festival at Worcester in 1902. As it was to take place in the Anglican cathedral, members of the festival committee insisted that the wording of some of the most Catholic verses be changed so as not to cause offence to non-Catholics. Fr Robert Eaton of the Birmingham Oratory, who had considerable experience as a choral conductor, wrote to Elgar:

> May I be allowed, as one who lives in the house where *Gerontius* was written, to again thank you for your superb setting of the poem – and to congratulate you very warmly on the rendering of your work last Thursday in Worcester? I was present and enjoyed it to the full. The intonation and quality of tone of the chorus were all one could wish – and surely Miss Foster is a true artist. I had heard the work mutilated at its first

production here – and do indeed rejoice that at last it has received a good rendering in England. I would like to go through the score some day with you to explain it more fully to me. I will pray that you may long be spared to write ...

The manuscript of the full score was presented by Elgar to the Fathers of the Oratory in Birmingham where the Cardinal had lived, worked and died; it can still be seen in Newman's library. In his letter to Fr Richard Bellasis, he wrote:

... nothing would give me greater happiness than to feel that the work, into which I put my whole soul, should be in its original form, near to where the sacred author of the poem made his influence felt.

Within a decade *The Dream* established itself with choral societies on a level with Handel's *Messiah* and Mendelssohn's *Elijah* and has been described as 'one of the great spiritual adventures of Romantic art'. The work has been specially associated with several distinguished conductors. In particular, Sir John Barbirolli directed performances throughout Britain, continental Europe, the USA and Australia. In 1958 he gave a performance of Part One at Castel Gandolfo, the summer residence of Pope Pius XII. As Barbirolli knelt for a blessing after the performance, the Pope said 'My son, that is a sublime masterpiece'. It was probably the last music that the Pope heard, as he died a few days later.

Elgar would have been well pleased with the superb centenary performance on 3rd October 2000 at the new Symphony Hall in Birmingham with the City of Birmingham Symphony Orchestra and Chorus under their Finnish conductor

Sakari Oramo. Unlike their predecessors in 1900, the chorus of over three hundred voices were so well rehearsed that they sang the work throughout from memory. Demand for tickets was such that the concert had to be repeated the following evening.

Denis Riches
Oxford, 6 January 2001

THE DREAM OF GERONTIUS

Praise to the Holiest in the height,
  and in the depth be praise,
In all His words most wonderful,
  most sure in all His ways.

To us, His elder race, He gave
  To battle and to win,
Without the chastisement of pain
  Without the soil of sin.

The
this younger son, ~~at His home,~~ He willed to be
  ^a a moment
  ~~young from~~ in his   birth,
Spirit and flesh his parents won,
  his home was heaven and earth.

The Eternal blessed this child, and armed,
  and sent him hence afar,
To serve as champion in the field
  Of elemental war.

Extract from Newman's manuscript

The Dream of Gerontius

I

GERONTIUS

JESU, MARIA — I am near to death,
   And thou art calling me; I know it now —
Not by the token of this faltering breath,
   This chill at heart, this dampness on my brow, —
Jesu, have mercy! Mary, pray for me! —
   'Tis this new feeling, never felt before,
Be with me, Lord, in my extremity!
   That I am going, that I am no more.
'Tis this strange innermost abandonment,
   Lover of souls! great God! I look to Thee,
This emptying out of each constituent
   And natural force, by which I come to be.
Pray for me, O my friends; a visitant
   Is knocking his dire summons at my door,
The like of whom, to scare me and to daunt,
   Has never, never come to me before;
'Tis death, — O loving friends, your prayers! — 'tis he!
   As though my very being had given way,
As though I was no more a substance now,
   And could fall back on nought to be my stay,

Help, loving Lord! Thou my sole Refuge, Thou,
   And turn no whither, but must needs decay
And drop from out this universal frame
   Into that shapeless, scopeless, blank abyss,
That utter nothingness, of which I came:
   This is it that has come to pass in me;
O horror! this it is, my dearest, this;
   So pray for me, my friends, who have not strength to pray.

ASSISTANTS

Kyrie eleïson, Christe eleïson, Kyrie eleïson.
Holy Mary, pray for him.
All holy Angels, pray for him.
Choirs of the righteous, pray for him.
Holy Abraham, pray for him.
St John Baptist, St Joseph, pray for him.
St Peter, St Paul, St Andrew, St John,
All Apostles, all Evangelists, pray for him.
All holy Disciples of the Lord, pray for him.
All holy Innocents, pray for him.
All holy Martyrs, all holy Confessors,
All holy Hermits, all holy Virgins,
All ye saints of God, pray for him.

GERONTIUS

Rouse thee, my fainting soul, and play the man;
  And through such waning span
Of life and thought as still has to be trod,
  Prepare to meet thy God.
And while the storm of that bewilderment
  Is for a season spent,
And, ere afresh the ruin on thee fall,
  Use well the interval.

ASSISTANTS

Be merciful, be gracious; spare him, Lord.
Be merciful, be gracious; Lord, deliver him
    From the sins that are past;
      From Thy frown and Thine ire;
    From the perils of dying;
      From any complying
    With sin, or denying
      His God, or relying
    On self, at the last;
      From the nethermost fire;
    From all that is evil;
      From power of the devil;
    Thy servant deliver,
      For once and for ever.

By Thy birth, and by Thy Cross,
 Rescue him from endless loss;
By Thy death and burial,
 Save him from a final fall;
By Thy rising from the tomb,
 By Thy mounting up above,
  By the Spirit's gracious love,
Save him in the day of doom.

GERONTIUS

Sanctus fortis, Sanctus Deus,
 De profundis oro te,
Miserere, Judex meus,
 Parce mihi, Domine.
Firmly I believe and truly
 God is Three, and God is One;
And I next acknowledge duly
 Manhood taken by the Son.
And I trust and hope most fully
 In that Manhood crucified;
And each thought and deed unruly
 Do to death, as He has died.
Simply to His grace and wholly
 Light and life and strength belong,
And I love, supremely, solely,
 Him the holy, Him the strong.

Sanctus fortis, Sanctus Deus,
De profundis oro te,
Miserere, Judex meus,
Parce mihi, Domine.
And I hold in veneration,
For the love of Him alone,
Holy Church, as His creation,
And her teachings, as His own.
And I take with joy whatever,
Now besets me, pain or fear,
And with a strong will I sever
All the ties which bind me here.
Adoration aye be given,
With and through the angelic host,
To the God of earth and Heaven,
Father, Son, and Holy Ghost.
Sanctus fortis, Sanctus Deus,
De profundis oro te,
Miserere, Judex meus,
Mortis in discrimine.

I can no more; for now it comes again,
That sense of ruin, which is worse than pain,
That masterful negation and collapse
Of all that makes me man; as though I bent
Over the dizzy brink
Of some sheer infinite descent;

Or worse, as though
Down, down for ever I was falling through
The solid framework of created things,
And needs must sink and sink
Into the vast abyss. And, crueller still,
A fierce and restless fright begins to fill
The mansion of my soul. And, worse and worse,
Some bodily form of ill.
Floats on the wind, with many a loathsome curse
Tainting the hallowed air, and laughs, and flaps
Its hideous wings,
And makes me wild with horror and dismay.
O Jesu, help! pray for me, Mary, pray!
Some angel, Jesu! such as came to Thee
In Thine own agony ...
Mary, pray for me. Joseph, pray for me.
Mary, pray for me.

ASSISTANTS

Rescue him, O Lord, in this his evil hour,
As of old so many by Thy gracious power: —
  Amen.
Enoch and Elias from the common doom;
  Amen.
Noe from the waters in a saving home;
  Amen.

Abraham from th'abounding guilt of Heathenesse;
   Amen.
Job from all his multiform and fell distress;
   Amen.
Isaac, when his father's knife was raised to slay;
   Amen.
Lot from burning Sodom on its judgment day;
   Amen.
Moses from the land of bondage and despair;
   Amen.
Daniel from the hungry lions in their lair;
   Amen.
And the children Three amid the fumace-flame;
   Amen.
Chaste Susanna from the slander and the shame;
   Amen.
David from Golia and the wrath of Saul;
   Amen.
And the two Apostles from their prison-thrall;
   Amen.
Thecla from her torments; Amen.
   – so, to show Thy power,
Rescue this Thy servant in his evil hour.

GERONTIUS

Novissima hora est; and I fain would sleep,
  The pain has wearied me ... Into Thy hands,
  O Lord, into Thy hands ...

THE PRIEST

Proficiscere, anima Christiana, de hoc mundo!
Go forth upon thy journey, Christian soul!
Go from this world! Go, in the name of God,
The omnipotent Father, who created thee!
Go, in the name of Jesus Christ, our Lord,
Son of the living God, who bled for thee!
Go, in the Name of the Holy Spirit, who
Hath been poured out on thee! Go, in the name
Of Angels and Archangels; in the name
Of Thrones and Dominations; in the name
Of Princedoms and of Powers; and in the name
Of Cherubim and Seraphim, go forth!
Go, in the name of Patriarchs and Prophets;
And of Apostles and Evangelists,
Of Martyrs and Confessors; in the name
Of holy Monks and Hermits; in the name
Of holy Virgins; and all Saints of God,
Both men and women, go! Go on thy course;
And may thy place to-day be found in peace,
And may thy dwelling be the Holy Mount
Of Sion: – through the Same, through Christ, our Lord.

II

SOUL OF GERONTIUS

I went to sleep; and now I am refreshed.
A strange refreshment: for I feel in me
An inexpressive lightness, and a sense
Of freedom, as I were at length myself,
And ne'er had been before. How still it is!
I hear no more the busy beat of time,
No, nor my fluttering breath, nor struggling pulse;
Nor does one moment differ from the next.
I had a dream; yes: — someone softly said
'He's gone'; and then a sigh went round the room.
And then I surely heard a priestly voice
Cry 'Subvenite'; and they knelt in prayer.
I seem to hear him still; but thin and low,
And fainter and more faint the accents come,
As at an ever-widening interval.
Ah! Whence is this? What is this severance?
This silence pours a solitariness
Into the very essence of my soul;
And the deep rest, so soothing and so sweet,
Hath something too of sternness and of pain,

For it drives back my thoughts upon their spring
By a strange introversion, and perforce
I now begin to feed upon myself,
Because I have nought else to feed upon.

Am I alive or dead? I am not dead,
But in the body still; for I possess
A sort of confidence which clings to me,
That each particular organ holds its place
As heretofore, combining with the rest
Into one symmetry, that wraps me round,
And makes me man; and surely I could move,
Did I but will it, every part of me.
And yet I cannot to my sense bring home,
By very trial, that I have the power
'Tis strange; I cannot stir a hand or foot,
I cannot make my fingers or my lips
By mutual pressure witness each to each,
Nor by the eyelid's instantaneous stroke
Assure myself I have a body still.
Nor do I know my very attitude,
Nor if I stand, or lie, or sit, or kneel.

So much I know, not knowing how I know,
That the vast universe, where I have dwelt,
Is quitting me, or I am quitting it,
Or I or it is rushing on the wings

Of light or lightning on an onward course,
And we e'en now are million miles apart.
Yet ... is this peremptory severance
Wrought out in lengthening measurements of space,
Which grow and multiply by speed and time?
Or am I traversing infinity
By endless subdivision, hurrying back
From finite towards infinitesimal,
Thus dying out of the expanded world?

Another marvel; someone has me fast
Within his ample palm; 'tis not a grasp
Such as they use on earth, but all around
Over the surface of my subtle being,
As though I were a sphere, and capable
To be accosted thus, a uniform
And gentle pressure tells me I am not
Self-moving, but borne forward on my way.
And hark! I hear a singing; yet in sooth
I cannot of that music rightly say
Whether I hear or touch or taste the tones.
Oh what a heart-subduing melody!

ANGEL

My work is done,
My task is o'er,
And so I come,
Taking it home,
For the crown is won,
Alleluia,
For evermore.

My Father gave
In charge to me
This child of earth
E'en from its birth,
To serve and save,
Alleluia,
And saved is he.

This child of clay
To me was given,
To rear and train
By sorrow and pain
In the narrow way,
Alleluia,
From earth to heaven.

SOUL

It is a member of that family
Of wondrous beings, who, ere the worlds were made,
Millions of ages back, have stood around
The throne of God: — he never has known sin;
But through those cycles all but infinite,
Has had a strong and pure celestial life,
And bore to gaze on th' unveiled face of God
And drank from the eternal Fount of truth,
And served Him with a keen ecstatic love.
Hark! he begins again.

ANGEL

O Lord, how wonderful in depth and height,
   But most in man, how wonderful Thou art!
With what a love, what soft persuasive might,
   Victorious o'er the stubborn fleshly heart,
  Thy tale complete of saints Thou dost provide,
  To fill the thrones which angels lost through pride!

He lay a grovelling babe upon the ground,
   Polluted in the blood of his first sire,
With his whole essence shattered and unsound,
   And, coiled around his heart, a demon dire,
  Which was not of his nature, but had skill
  To bind and form his opening mind to ill.

Then was I sent from heaven to set right
    The balance in his soul of truth and sin,
And I have waged a long relentless fight,
    Resolved that death-environed spirit to win,
  Which from its fallen state, when all was lost,
  Had been repurchased at so dread a cost.

O what a shifting parti-coloured scene
    Of hope and fear, of triumph and dismay,
Of recklessness and penitence, has been
    The history of that dreary, lifelong fray!
  And O the grace to nerve him and to lead,
  How patient, prompt, and lavish at his need!

O man, strange composite of heaven and earth!
    Majesty dwarfed to baseness! fragrant flower
Running to poisonous seed! and seeming worth
    Cloking corruption! weakness mastering power!
  Who never art so near to crime and shame,
  As when thou hast achieved some deed of name; —

How should ethereal natures comprehend
    A thing made up of spirit and of clay,
Were we not tasked to nurse it and to tend,
    Linked one to one throughout its mortal day?
  More than the Seraph in his height of place,
  The Angel-guardian knows and loves the ransomed race.

SOUL

Now know I surely that I am at length
Out of the body: had I part with earth,
I never could have drunk those accents in,
And not have worshipped as a god the voice
That was so musical; but now I am
So whole of heart, so calm, so self-possessed,
With such a full content, and with a sense
So apprehensive and discriminant,
As no temptation can intoxicate.
Nor have I even terror at the thought
That I am clasped by such a saintliness.

ANGEL

All praise to Him, at whose sublime decree
    The last are first, the first become the last;
By whom the suppliant prisoner is set free,
    By whom proud first-borns from their thrones are cast;
    Who raises Mary to be Queen of heaven,
    While Lucifer is left, condemned and unforgiven.

III

SOUL

I will address him. Mighty one, my Lord,
My Guardian Spirit, all hail!

ANGEL

   All hail, my child!
My child and brother, hail! what wouldest thou?

SOUL

I would have nothing but to speak with thee
For speaking's sake. I wish to hold with thee
Conscious communion; though I fain would know.
 A maze of things, were it but meet to ask,
And not a curiousness.

ANGEL

   You cannot now
Cherish a wish which ought not to be wished.

SOUL

Then I will speak. I ever had believed
That on the moment when the struggling soul
Quitted its mortal case, forthwith it fell
Under the awful Presence of its God,
There to be judged and sent to its own place.
What lets me now from going to my Lord?

ANGEL

Thou art not let; but with extremest speed
Art hurrying to the just and Holy judge:
For scarcely art thou disembodied yet.
Divide a moment, as men measure time,
Into its million-million-millionth part,
Yet even less than that the interval
Since thou didst leave the body; and the priest
Cried 'Subvenite', and they fell to prayer;
Nay, scarcely yet have they begun to pray.

For spirits and men by different standards mete
The less and greater in the flow of time.
By sun and moon, primeval ordinances –
By stars which rise and set harmoniously –
By the recurring seasons, and the swing,
This way and that, of the suspended rod

Precise and punctual, men divide the hours,
Equal, continuous, for their common use.
Not so with us in th' immaterial world;
But intervals in their succession
Are measured by the living thought alone,
And grow or wane with its intensity.
And time is not a common property;
But what is long is short, and swift is slow,
And near is distant, as received and grasped
By this mind and by that, and every one
Is standard of his own chronology.
And memory lacks its natural resting–points
Of years, and centuries, and periods.
It is thy very energy of thought
Which keeps thee from thy God.

SOUL

          Dear Angel, say,
Why have I now no fear at meeting Him?
Along my earthly life, the thought of death
And judgment was to me most terrible.
I had it aye before me, and I saw
The Judge severe e'en in the crucifix.

Now that the hour is come, my fear is fled;
And at this balance of my destiny,
Now close upon me, I can forward look
With a serenest joy.

ANGEL

It is because
Then thou didst fear, that now thou dost not fear.
Thou hast forestalled the agony, and so
For thee the bitterness of death is past.
Also, because already in thy soul
The judgment is begun. That day of doom,
One and the same for the collected world, —
That solemn consummation for all flesh,
Is, in the case of each, anticipate
Upon his death; and, as the last great day
In the particular judgment is rehearsed,
So now too, ere thou comest to the throne,
A presage falls upon thee, as a ray
Straight from the Judge, expressive of thy lot.
That calm and joy uprising in thy soul
Is first-fruit to thee of thy recompense,
And heaven begun.

IV

SOUL

        But hark! upon my sense
Comes a fierce hubbub, which would make me fear,
Could I be frighted.

ANGEL

         We are now arrived
Close on the judgment court; that sullen howl
Is from the demons who assemble there.
It is the middle region, where of old
Satan appeared among the sons of God,
To cast his jibes and scoffs at holy Job.
So now his legions throng the vestibule,
Hungry and wild, to claim their property,
And gather souls for hell. Hist to their cry.

SOUL

How sour and how uncouth a dissonance!

DEMONS

Low-born clods
  Of brute earth,
    They aspire
To become gods,
  By a new birth,
And an extra grace,
  And a score of merits,
    As if aught
Could stand in place
  Of the high thought,
  And the glance of fire
Of the great spirits,
The powers blest,
  The Lords by right,
    The primal owners
    Of the proud dwelling
And realm of light,
Dispossessed,
Aside thrust,
    Chucked down,
  By the sheer might
Of a despot's will,
  Of a tyrant's frown,
  Who after expelling
Their hosts, gave,
Triumphant still,

45

And still unjust,
    Each forfeit crown
To psalm-droners,
And canting groaners
    To every slave,
And pious cheat,
And crawling knave,
Who licked the dust
    Under his feet.

ANGEL

It is the restless panting of their being;
Like beasts of prey, who, caged within their bars,
In a deep hideous purring have their life,
And an incessant pacing to and fro.

DEMONS

The mind bold
  And independent,
The purpose free,
So we are told,
Must not think
  To have the ascendant.
    What's a saint?
One whose breath

Doth the air taint
Before his death;
A bundle of bones,
Which fools adore,
Ha! ha!
When life is o'er,
Which rattle and stink,
E'en in the flesh.
We cry his pardon!
No flesh hath he;
Ha! ha!
For it hath died,
'Tis crucified
Day by day,
Afresh, afresh,
Ha! ha!
That holy clay,
Ha! ha!
And such fudge,
As priestlings prate,
Is his guerdon
Before the Judge,
And pleads and atones
For spite and grudge,
And bigot mood,
And envy and hate,
And greed of blood.

SOUL

How impotent they are! and yet on earth
They have repute for wondrous power and skill;
And books describe, how that the very face
Of th' Evil One, if seen, would have a force
To freeze the very blood, and choke the life
Of him who saw it.

ANGEL

       In thy trial-state
Thou hadst a traitor nestling close at home,
Connatural, who with the powers of hell
Was leagued, and of thy senses kept the keys,
And to that deadliest foe unlocked thy heart.
And therefore is it, in respect of man,
Those fallen ones show so majestical.
But, when some child of grace, angel or saint,
Pure and upright in his integrity
Of nature, meets the demons on their raid,
They scud away as cowards from the fight.
Nay, oft hath holy hermit in his cell,
Not yet disburdened of mortality,
Mocked at their threats and warlike overtures;
Or, dying, when they swarmed, like flies, around,
Defied them, and departed to his Judge.

DEMONS

Virtue and vice,
  A knave's pretence,
  'Tis all the same;
    Ha! ha!
Dread of hell-fire,
  Of the venomous name,
  A coward's plea.
Give him his price,
  Saint though he be,
    Ha! ha!
From shrewd good sense
  He'll slave for hire;
    Ha! ha!
And does but aspire
To the heaven above
  With sordid aim,
  And not from love.
    Ha! ha!

SOUL

I see not those false spirits; shall I see
My dearest Master, when I reach His throne;
Or hear, at least, His awful judgment-word
With personal intonation, as I now

Hear thee, not see thee Angel? Hitherto
All has been darkness since I left the earth;
Shall I remain thus sight-bereft all through
My penance time? If so, how comes it then
That I have hearing still, and taste, and touch,
Yet not a glimmer of that princely sense
Which binds ideas in one, and makes them live?

ANGEL

Nor touch, nor taste, nor hearing hast thou now;
Thou livest in a world of signs and types,
The presentations of most holy truths,
Living and strong, which now encompass thee.
A disembodied soul, thou hast by right
No converse with aught else beside thyself;
But, lest so stern a solitude should load
And break thy being, in mercy are vouchsafed
Some lower measures of perception,
Which seem to thee, as though through channels brought,
Through ear, or nerves, or palate, which are gone.
And thou art wrapped and swathed around in dreams,
Dreams that are true, yet enigmatical;
For the belongings of thy present state,
Save through such symbols, come not home to thee.
And thus thou tell'st of space, and time, and size,
Of fragrant, solid, bitter, musical,
Of fire, and of refreshment after fire;

As (let me use similitude of earth,
To aid thee in the knowledge thou dost ask) —
As ice which blisters may be said to burn.
Nor hast thou now extension, with its parts
Correlative, — long habit cozens thee, —
Nor power to move thyself, nor limbs to move.
Hast thou not heard of those, who, after loss
Of hand or foot, still cried that they had pains
In hand or foot, as though they had it still?
So is it now with thee, who hast not lost
Thy hand or foot, but all which made up man;
So will it be, until the joyous day
Of resurrection, when thou wilt regain
All thou hast lost, new-made and glorified.
How, even now, the consummated Saints
See God in heaven, I may not explicate.
Meanwhile let it suffice thee to possess
Such means of converse as are granted thee,
Though, till that Beatific Vision thou art blind;
For e'en thy purgatory, which comes like fire,
Is fire without its light.

SOUL

                His will be done!
I am not worthy e'er to see again
The face of day; far less His countenance,

Who is the very sun. Natheless, in life,
When I looked forward to my purgatory,
It ever was my solace to believe
That, ere I plunged into th' avenging flame,
I had one sight of Him to strengthen me.

ANGEL

Nor rash nor vain is that presentiment;
Yes, – for one moment thou shalt see thy Lord.
Thus will it be: what time thou art arraigned
Before the dread tribunal, and thy lot
Is cast for ever, should it be to sit
On His right hand among His pure elect,
Then sight, or that which to the soul is sight,
As by a lightning-flash, will come to thee,
And thou shalt see, amid the dark profound,
Whom thy soul loveth, and would fain approach,
One moment; but thou knowest not, my child,
What thou dost ask: that sight of the Most Fair
Will gladden thee, but it will pierce thee too.

SOUL

Thou speakest darkly, Angel; and an awe
Falls on me, and a fear lest I be rash.

ANGEL

There was a mortal, who is now above
In the mid glory: he, when near to die,
Was given communion with the Crucified, –
Such, that the Master's very wounds were stamped
Upon his flesh; and from the agony
Which thrilled through body and soul in that embrace
Learn that the flame of the Everlasting Love
Doth burn ere it transform . . .

V

        Hark to those sounds!
They come of tender beings angelical,
Least and most childlike of the sons of God.

FIRST CHOIR OF ANGELICALS

Praise to the Holiest in the height,
   And in the depth be praise:
In all His words most wonderful;
   Most sure in all His ways!

To us His elder race He gave
   To battle and to win,
Without the chastisement of pain,
   Without the soil of sin.

The younger son He willed to be
   A marvel in his birth:
Spirit and flesh his parents were;
   His home was heaven and earth.

The Eternal blessed His child, and armed,
  And sent him hence afar
To serve as champion in the field
  Of elemental war.

To be His Viceroy in the world
  Of matter, and of sense;
Upon the frontier, towards the foe,
  A resolute defence.

ANGEL

We now have passed the gate, and are within
The House of Judgment; and whereas on earth
Temples and palaces are formed of parts
Costly and rare, but all material,
So in the world of spirits nought is found,
To mould withal and form into a whole,
But what is immaterial; and thus
The smallest portions of this edifice,
Cornice, or frieze, or balustrade, or stair,
The very pavement is made up of life —
Of holy, blessed, and immortal beings,
Who hymn their Maker's praise continually.

Praise to the Holiest in the height,
   And in the depth be praise:
In all His words most wonderful;
   Most sure in all His ways!

Woe to thee, man; for he was found
   A recreant in the fight;
And lost his heritage of heaven,
   And fellowship with light.

Above him now the angry sky
   Around the tempest's din;
Who once had angels for his friends,
   Has but the brutes for kin.

O man! a savage kindred they:
   To flee that monster brood
He scaled the seaside cave, and clomb
   The giants of the wood.

With now a fear, and now a hope,
   With aids which chance supplied,
From youth to old, from sire to son,
   He lived, and toiled and died.

He dreed his penance age by age;
  And step by step began
Slowly to doff his savage garb
  And be again a man.

And quickened by the Almighty's breath,
  And chastened by His rod,
And taught by Angel-visitings,
  At length he sought his God:

And learned to call upon His name,
  And in His faith create
A household and a fatherland,
  A city and a state.

Glory to Him who from the mire,
  In patient length of days,
Elaborated into life
  A people to His praise!

SOUL

The sound is like the rushing of the wind –
The summer wind - among the lofty pines;
Swelling and dying, echoing round about,
Now here, now distant, wild and beautiful;
While, scattered from the branches it has stirred,
Descend ecstatic odours.

THIRD CHOIR OF ANGELICALS

Praise to the Holiest in the height,
  And in the depth be praise:
In all His words most wonderful;
  Most sure in all His ways!

The Angels, as beseemingly
  To spirit-kind was given,
At once were tried and perfected,
  And took their seats in heaven.

For them no twilight or eclipse;
  No growth and no decay:
'Twas hopeless, all-ingulfing night,
  Or beatific day.

But to the younger race there rose
  A hope upon its fall;
And slowly, surely, gracefully,
  The morning dawned on all.

And ages, opening out, divide
  The precious and the base,
And from the hard and sullen mass,
  Mature the heirs of grace.

O man! albeit the quickening ray,
　Lit from his second birth,
Makes him at length what once he was,
　And heaven grows out of earth;

Yet still between that earth and heaven –
　His journey and his goal –
A double agony awaits
　His body and his soul.

A double debt he has to pay –
　The forfeit of his sins,
The chill of death is past, and now
　The penance-fire begins.

Glory to Him, who evermore
　By truth and justice reigns;
Who tears the soul from out its case,
　And burns away its stains!

ANGEL

They sing of thy approaching agony,
Which thou so eagerly didst question of:
It is the face of the Incarnate God
Shall smite thee with that keen and subtle pain;

And yet the memory which it leaves will be
A sovereign febrifuge to heal the wound;
And yet withal it will the wound provoke,
And aggravate and widen it the more.

SOUL

Thou speakest mysteries; still methinks I know
To disengage the tangle of thy words:
Yet rather would I hear thy angel voice,
Than for myself be thy interpreter.

ANGEL

When then – if such thy lot – thou seest thy Judge,
The sight of Him will kindle in thy heart,
All tender, gracious, reverential thoughts.
Thou wilt be sick with love, and yearn for Him,
And feel as though thou couldst but pity Him,
That one so sweet should e'er have placed Himself
At disadvantage such, as to be used
So vilely by a being so vile as thee.
There is a pleading in His pensive eyes
Will pierce thee to the quick, and trouble thee.
And thou wilt hate and loathe thyself; for, though
Now sinless, thou wilt feel that thou hast sinned,

As never thou didst feel; and wilt desire
To slink away, and hide thee from His sight;
And yet wilt have a longing aye to dwell
Within the beauty of His countenance.
And these two pains, so counter and so keen, –
The longing for Him, when thou seest Him not;
The shame of self at thought of seeing Him, –
Will be thy veriest, sharpest purgatory.

SOUL

My soul is in my hand: I have no fear, –
In His dear might prepared for weal or woe.
But hark! a deep mysterious harmony:
It floods me, like the deep and solemn sound
Of many waters.

ANGEL

      We have gained the stairs
Which rise towards the Presence-chamber; there
A band of mighty Angels keep the way
One either side, and hymn the Incarnate God.

Father, whose goodness none can know, but they
  Who see Thee face to face,
By man hath come the infinite display
  Of Thine all-loving grace;
But fallen man – the creature of a day –
  Skills not that love to trace.
It needs, to tell the triumph Thou hast wrought,
An Angel's deathless fire, an Angel's reach of thought.

It needs that very angel, who with awe,
  Amid the garden shade,
The great Creator in His sickness saw,
  Soothed by a creature's aid,
And agonised, as victim of the Law
  Which He Himself had made;
For who can praise Him in His depth and height,
But he who saw Him reel amid that solitary fight?

SOUL

Hark! for the lintels of the presence-gate
Are vibrating and echoing back the strain.

FOURTH CHOIR OF ANGELICALS

Praise to the Holiest in the height,
  And in the depths be praise:
In all His words most wonderful;
  Most sure in all His ways!

The foe blasphemed the Holy Lord,
  As if He reckoned ill,
In that He placed His puppet man
  The frontier place to fill.

For even in his best estate,
  With amplest gifts endued,
A sorry sentinel was he,
  A being of flesh and blood.

As though a thing, who for his help
  Must needs possess a wife,
Could cope with those proud rebel hosts,
  Who had angelic life.

And when, by blandishment of Eve,
  That earth-born Adam fell,
He shrieked in triumph, and he cried,
  'A sorry sentinel.

The Maker by His word is bound
  Escape or cure is none;
He must abandon to his doom,
  And slay His darling son.'

ANGEL

And now the threshold, as we traverse it,
Utters aloud its glad responsive chant.

FIFTH CHOIR OF ANGELICALS

Praise to the Holiest in the height,
  And in the depth be praise:
In all His words most wonderful;
  Most sure in all His ways!

O loving wisdom of our God!
  When all was sin and shame,
A second Adam to the fight
  And to the rescue came.

O wisest love! that flesh and blood
  Which did in Adam fail,
Should strive afresh against the foe,
  Should strive and should prevail.

And that a higher gift than grace
   Should flesh and blood refine,
God's presence and His very Self,
   And Essence all-divine.

O generous love! that He who smote
   In man for man the foe,
The double agony in man.
   For man should undergo;

And in the garden secretly,
   And on the cross on high,
Should teach His brethren and inspire
   To suffer and to die.

VI

ANGEL

Thy judgment now is near, for we are come
Into the veiled presence of our God.

SOUL

I hear the voices that I left on earth.

ANGEL

It is the voice of friends around thy bed,
Who say the 'Subvenite' with the priest.
Hither the echoes come; before the Throne
Stands the great Angel of the Agony,
The same who strengthened Him, what time He knelt
Lone in the garden shade, bedewed with blood.
That Angel best can plead with Him for all
Tormented souls, the dying and the dead.

ANGEL OF THE AGONY

Jesu! by that shuddering dread which fell on Thee;
Jesu! by that cold dismay which sickened Thee;
Jesu! by that pang of heart which thrilled in Thee;
Jesu! by that mount of sins which crippled Thee;
Jesu! by that sense of guilt which stifled Thee;
Jesu! by that innocence which girdled Thee;
Jesu! by that sanctity which reigned in Thee;
Jesu! by that Godhead which was one with Thee;
Jesu! spare these souls which are so dear to Thee;
Who in prison, calm and patient, wait for Thee;
Hasten, Lord, their hour, and bid them come to Thee,
To that glorious Home, where they shall ever gaze on Thee.

SOUL

I go before my Judge.

ANGEL

        ... Praise to His name!
The eager spirit has darted from my hold,
And, with the intemperate energy of love,
Flies to the dear feet of Emmanuel;
But, ere it reach them, the keen sanctity,

Which with its effluence, like a glory, clothes
And circles round the Crucified, has seized,
And scorched, and shrivelled it; and now it lies
Passive and still before the awful Throne.
O happy, suffering soul! for it is safe,
Consumed, yet quickened, by the glance of God.

SOUL

Take me away, and in the lowest deep
   There let me be,
And there in hope the lone night-watches keep,
   Told out for me.
There, motionless and happy in my pain,
   Lone, not forlorn, –
There will I sing my sad perpetual strain,
   Until the morn.
There will I sing, and soothe my stricken breast,
   Which ne'er can cease
To throb, and pine, and languish, till possest
   Of its Sole Peace.
There will I sing my absent Lord and Love: –
   Take me away,
That sooner I may rise, and go above,
   And see Him in the truth of everlasting day.

VII

ANGEL

Now let the golden prison ope its gates,
Making sweet music, as each fold revolves
Upon its ready hinge. And ye, great powers,
Angels of Purgatory, receive from me
My charge, a precious soul, until the day,
When, from all bond and forfeiture released,
I shall reclaim it for the courts of light.

SOULS IN PURGATORY

Lord, Thou hast been our refuge: in every generation;

Before the hills were born, and the world was:
   from age to age Thou art God.

Bring us not, Lord, very low: for Thou hast said,
   Come back again, ye sons of Adam.

A thousand years before Thine eyes are but as yesterday:
   and as a watch of the night which is come and gone.

The grass springs up in the morning;
at evening-tide it shrivels up and dies.

So we fail in Thine anger; and in Thy wrath are we troubled.

Thou hast set our sins in Thy sight:
  and our round of days in the light of Thy countenance.

Come back, O Lord! how long?
  and be entreated for Thy servants.

In Thy morning we shall be filled with Thy mercy:
  we shall rejoice and be in pleasure all our days.

We shall be glad according to the days of our humiliation;
  and the years in which we have seen evil.

Look, O Lord, upon Thy servants and on Thy work:
  and direct their children.

And let the beauty of the Lord our God be upon us:
  and the work of our hands, establish Thou it.

  Glory be to the Father, and to the Son;
  And to the Holy Ghost.
  As it was in the beginning, is now, and ever shall be:
  World without end. Amen.

ANGEL

Softly and gently, dearest, sweetest soul,
  In my most loving arms I now enfold thee,
And, o'er the penal waters, as they roll,
  I poise thee, and I lower thee, and hold thee.

And carefully I dip thee in the lake,
  And though, without a sob or a resistance,
Dost through the flood thy rapid passage take,
  Sinking deep, deeper, into the dim distance.

Angels, to whom the willing task is given,
  Shall tend, and nurse, and lull thee, as thou liest;
And Masses on the earth, and prayers in heaven,
  Shall aid thee at the Throne of the Most Highest.

Farewell, but not for ever! brother dear,
  Be brave and patient on thy bed of sorrow;
Swiftly shall pass thy night of trial here,
  And I will come and wake thee on the morrow.

The title page of the autograph full score of *The Dream*.
At bottom right is Richter's memorable inscription to the
composer, 'Let drop the Chorus, let drop everybody –
but let *not* drop the wings of your original genius'.

DISCOGRAPHY

The Dream of Gerontius by Sir Edward Elgar

Huddersfield Choral Society & Liverpool Philharmonic Orchestra
conducted by Sir Malcolm Sargent
Heddle Nash, tenor; Gladys Ripley, mezzo-soprano;
Dennis Noble, baritone; Norman Walker, bass
    (also Elgar: *'Cello concerto*; Paul Tortelier & BBC Symphony Orchestra)
Testament Mon SBT 2025 (2)   (1945)

Huddersfield Choral Society & Royal Liverpool Philharmonic Orchestra
conducted by Sir Malcolm Sargent
Richard Lewis, tenor; Marjorie Thomas, mezzo; John Cameron, bass
    (also Walton: *Belshazzar's Feast* with James Milligan, baritone (1958))
CHS 7 63376 2 (2)   (1964)

Hallé & Sheffield Philharmonic Chorus & Ambrosian Singers
Hallé Orchestra conducted by Sir John Barbirolli
Richard Lewis, tenor; Janet Baker, mezzo-soprano; Kim Borg, bass
    (also Elgar: *Sea Pictures*, with Janet Baker)
EMI CMS 7 63185 2 (2)   (1964)

London Symphony Chorus, Choir of Kings College, Cambridge
London Symphony Orchestra conducted by Benjamin Britten
Peter Pears, Tenor; Yvonne Minton, mezzo;
John Shirley-Quirk, bass   (1972)
  (also Holst's *The Hymn of Jesus*, op 37)
BBC Symphony Orchestra & Chorus with Sir Adrian Boult   (1962)
Decca/London 421 381-2

John Aldis Choir & London Philharmonic Chorus
New Philharmonic Orchestra conducted by Sir Adrian Boult
Nicolai Gedda, Tenor; Helen Watts, mezzo; Robert Lloyd, bass   (1975)
    (also Elgar's *The Music Makers*, op 69 with Janet Baker
    London Philharmonic Chorus with Sir Adrian Boult (1966))
EMI CMS5 66540 (2)

City of Birmingham Chorus & Symphony Orchestra
conducted by Sir Simon Rattle
John Mitchinson, tenor; Janet Baker, mezzo; John Shirley-Quirk, bass
CSS 7 49549 2 (2)   (1987)

London Symphony Chorus & Orchestra conducted by Richard Hickox
Arthur Davies, tenor; Felicity Palmer, mezzo-soprano; Robert Lloyd, bass
    (also Parry: *Anthems*)
Chandos 8641/2   (1988)

Royal Scottish National Orchestra & Chorus
conducted by Sir Alexander Gibson
Robert Tear, tenor; Alfreda Hodgson, mezzo; Benjamin Luxon, bass
CRD 33267   (1976)

Liverpool Philharmonic Choir, Huddersfield Choral Society
Royal Liverpool Philharmonic Orchestra conducted by Vernon Handley
Anthony Rolfe Johnson, tenor; Catherine Wyn-Rogers, contralto;
Michael George, bass
HMV D5727582   (1993)

Bournemouth Symphony Chorus, Waynflete Singers
Bournemouth Symphony Orchestra conducted by David Hill
William Kendall, tenor; Sarah Fryer, mezzo-soprano; Matthew Best, bass
Naxos 85538856   (1996)

BBC Symphony Chorus & Orchestra conducted by Andrew Davis
Philip Langridge, tenor; Catherine Wyn-Rogers, mezzo; Alastair Milne, bass
(BBC video of performance at St Pauls Cathedral, London; 1998)
NVC Arts 3984223513   (1998)